S≠XY GiRls

How Hot Is Too Hot?

S≠XY GiRls

How Hot Is Too Hot?

HAYLEY DIMARCO

Revell
Grand Rapids, Michigan

Hungry Planet

© 2006 by Hungry Planet

Published by Revell
a division of Baker Publishing Group
P.O. Box 6287, Grand Rapids, MI 49516-6287
www.revellbooks.com

Fourth printing, December 2008

Printed in the United States of America

Library of Congress Cataloging-in-Publication Data
DiMarco, Hayley.
    Sexy girls : how hot is too hot? / Hayley DiMarco.
       p.   cm.
       ISBN 10: 0-8007-3084-4 (pbk.)
       ISBN 978-0-8007-3084-0 (pbk.)
         1. Teenage girls—Conduct of life—Juvenile literature.
      2. Teenage girls—Religious life—Juvenile literature. I. Title.
    BJ1651.D56 2006
    248.8′33—dc22   2005033762

Published in association with Yates & Yates, LLP, Literary Agents, Orange, California.

Contents

INTRODUCTION

You might not claim to be sexy. You might not even want to be sexy. But if you're a normal, red-blooded girl, then I bet you want to be attractive to the opposite sex. You want the attention of guys, and you do certain things to get it. You wear that cute baby doll top. You pick jeans that make you look just so. You know exactly what to wear to accentuate your good parts. It's natural, you know, to want to attract the opposite sex. The trouble is that sometimes we don't really realize what we are doing to the opposite sex in this dance for attention. *Sexy Girls* is all about helping you understand your body and how guys look at it. It's not an attempt to tell you not to be cute and stylish and hip. And it's not an attempt to make you a sexy bombshell. But it *is* a place for you to start to better understand your sexuality and how it impacts the guys around you.

I want you to be the best that you can be, and I won't ask you to join the army to do that. But I will ask you to consider how you are currently dressing and acting and to think about how you might want to change to create a better overall package that fits your life goals. *Sexy Girls* is a book that will help you better define who you are and how you can attract the opposite sex without losing sight of your faith and your commitment to purity. So are you ready to find out how hot is too hot?

"It's hard to speak to your hearts when all I see is your parts."

—Confessions of a Youth Pastor

chapter 1

CREATING THE PERFECT IMAGE

"So who's your agent?"

What is sexy? Are you? Do you wanna be? Should you be sexy? And ultimately what is the goal of being sexy?

On my first day of first grade, my mom let me pick out my outfit. It was the end of summer, so I had all these cute summer clothes that I still loved. I chose a cool little outfit that was made of a little bitty skirt and a top that was really short, like a bathing suit top. I was only five, remember, so all I thought about was how much I liked that outfit. I was a clotheshorse even then.

Well, when I got to school and got into my classroom, a memory became forever etched in my head. My teacher took me aside and told me to go to the principal's office. I was improperly dressed, and my mom needed to come get me. I remember being completely embarrassed. Would I forever be the outsider now that I had made the fatal mistake of misdressing? I mean, I was five, how was I to know what was appropriate for school and what wasn't? My sole goal was to wear my favorite outfit, and so that's what I did, without having a clue that it was inappropriate for school. Ah, the tragedy of youth!

Things didn't get much better from there. My sophomore year in high school, I decided that it was time for a change. Up until then I was the nerd. I wore two long, blond pigtails every day. And I only wore pink. Every single day of my life, only pink. But my sophomore year I got tired of being the fluffy pink geek, so I went for a more sexy look. I wasn't trying to be a sex queen or anything. I just wanted to be cute and to be thought of as hip. So I hit the stores running.

My mom gave me $400 to revamp my wardrobe, and that's what I did. I remember the first day of school that sophomore year—suddenly all the guys were looking at me. They had never looked at me before. I was suddenly in, or so I thought. I was now the hip dresser. Styles were different then, of course, but they were still designed to make girls sexy. And so I became, without giving much thought to the ramifications, a sexy girl. I started on a kind of campaign to remake my image, but the trouble was that I didn't really realize what I was now advertising. My newfound sexiness did get the attention of many a boy, but then what? I didn't know what to do with it. So I got labeled a tease (more on that later). I had advertised something I couldn't deliver. Trouble was, no one explained sexiness to me. I had no idea what it was doing to the guys in my rearview mirror. I didn't know the message I was sending. Let's face it, I was clueless when it came to sexy.

Sexy, according to Webster's

dictionary, is "something that is sexually suggestive or stimulating." So if you're looking sexy, don't be surprised when guys get that drooling, glazed-over look.

In Hollywood every starlet knows you have to have an image consultant.

You have to hire someone who will help you craft an image that you want the rest of the world to buy. You want the world to get who you are as a star by how you dress, where you go, and who you are seen with. An image consultant, together with a PR agent, is the starlet's best friend.

But starlets aren't the only ones who have an image to sell. Every day, whether you know it or not, you put together your own PR package. You decide every morning what image you want the rest of the world to see in you. You say to yourself, *Fancy or casual? Sporty or revealing?* You make choices that define your image. Everyone has one—an image, that is. And if you don't get it yet, think about it like this.

Think about all your friends, enemies, acquaintances. Think about all the girls you know, and then start to think about what image they project. Your image is what other people think about you when you aren't around. It's that impression you leave them with when you walk out of the room. And everyone has one. Whether you show up buttoned up and covered up or looking like you just jumped into the laundry basket and came out all dressed, you project an image that other people are picking up on. Like most people, you probably don't have the benefit of a full-time image consultant, but hold on, because *Sexy Girls* is comin' to the rescue! I want to help you figure out your image—who you are, who you want to be, and who you want others to think you are. After that we'll craft a look that will present you to the rest of the world just the way you want to be presented. Your PR agent will be yourself. No exorbitant fees! No kissing up to you because you're loaded! Just a great PR package that will help you define who you are and how you want others to respond to you.

MARKETING 101

See, it's all about marketing. Just like Sprite or A&F have a certain image that they want their target market to get, so each one of us has an image we want our target market to get. For most of you, your target is the male population at your school. Maybe when you were younger, your target audience was your best friends. Either way, every day when you get dressed, you create an image and marketing campaign that tells your target market what they get when they "get" you. Are you hot, sassy, playful, exciting, shy, seductive, or athletic? As I've said, you've probably never really thought about this accidental marketing, but you do it. So why not take charge of your marketing campaign and make it what you want it to be and not some big accident—or one waiting to happen? Let's start off with a little image consulting. This is the prep work we need to do before we dive into "what sexy really is" and how we manage our own sexiness.

IMAGE CONSULTING

Before we get started, let's define your current image. What do you say to the rest of the world, either intentionally or accidentally, by the way you dress? This is the fun part! Look at these pics and circle the one that's the most like you most of the time.

  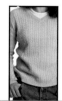  

If you could identify with any of these styles, then you already have the makings of an image. Now ask yourself a few questions before we dive into the total image analysis (and maybe even makeover) that you might be screaming for right now. *Sexy Girls* is your chance to figure out who you want the rest of the world to see and then to figure out how to create that image. You aren't at the mercy of anyone when it comes to your image. You might need to give it a little creativity and energy, but you can make an image that you'll be proud of and that will really portray who you are. So before we dive into what's sexy and what's not, let's have a look at you.

First, pick three adjectives that describe who you are and who you want others to see in you:

Funny	Playful	Athletic	Smart	Casual
Sexy	Flirtatious	Hard to Get	Easy	Valuable
Spiritual	Confident	Conservative	Quirky	Creative

Okay, now let's look at your style. Do you want to be (circle up to three):

Artsy	Stylish	Traditional	Goth	Preppie
Athletic	Trendy	Revealing	Sexual	Brainy
Other: _____				

When it comes to what people see, do they think of you as (circle one from each line):

Experimental	or	Conservative
Worldly	or	Innocent
Traditional	or	Daring
Romantic	or	Purely Physical

When it comes to your spiritual life, do you want to be thought of as (circle one from each line):

Spiritual   or   Nonspiritual
Godly   or   Worldly
Open-Minded or   Traditional

When it comes to your social life, are you more likely to:

Stay up late with friends   or   Stay up late with your books
Date around   or   Date one guy exclusively
Sneak out of the house late   or   Go to bed early

If you could have the life of any starlet, who would it be?

_____

You might be wondering why all the self-analysis, but I'm not going to tell you just yet. You'll refer back to this section later on in the book. So for now, good work. Hope you were honest, because it's really hard to create an image that fits if you are lying to yourself about who you are.

HOW SEXY ARE YOU?

1. **Most of my tops don't come all the way to my pants.**
   True   False

2. **I think it's okay to show a little bit of my stomach.**
   True   False

3. **I don't have any tops that show my cleavage.**   True   False

4. **I have at least one body piercing.**   True   False

5. **I think tattoos are cute and sexy.**   True   False

6. **I dress in what I think is cute. My goal isn't to get the attention of guys.**   True   False

7. **I like it when guys look at my chest.**   True   False

8. **My parents keep telling me I dress too sexy.**   True   False

9. **I try to buy tops that aren't too revealing.**   True   False

10. **I think it's hard to find clothes that aren't too sexy.**
    True   False

1. True = 2, False = 1 _____
2. True = 2, False = 1 _____
3. True = 1, False = 2 _____
4. True = 2, False = 1 _____
5. True = 2, False = 1 _____
6. True = 1, False = 2 _____
7. True = 2, False = 1 _____
8. True = 2, False = 1 _____
9. True = 1, False = 2 _____
10. True = 1, False = 2 _____

Your score: _____

20–17: You're Hot. And everyone knows it! You definitely have a sexy edge about you. You might not be aware of it, but you are turning on guys right and left. Read on and find out why. You might just start to rethink things.

16–14: Sexy Sometimes. I bet you turn a few heads some of the time. It's not 'cuz you're having a good hair day. They like looking at the body you've got showing. If you don't realize how your sex appeal is affecting guys, you soon will.

13–10: Can Anyone Say Cute? You think carefully about how you look and care what guys are thinking about your body. It looks like you've learned the power of your flesh and are using it wisely. Well done.

Your Accidental Image

chapter 2

YOUR TARGET MARKET

What are guys thinking?

QUIZ

GUYS AND SEXY

Let's see what you know about guys and sexy:

1. Guys think about sex:
- a. several times a day
- b. whenever they see a little flesh
- c. no more than girls do
- d. both a and b

2. Guys are turned on by:
- a. the girl they like
- b. all girls
- c. girls who show their cleavage
- d. all of the above

3. Guys are easily excited by what:
- a. they hear
- b. they see
- c. they do

4. Guys think that if you are showing midriff, you are:
- a. a really cute dresser
- b. easy
- c. looking for attention
- d. a sexual girl
- e. b, c, and d

1. a = 2, b = 2, c = 1, d = 3
2. a = 1, b = 2, c = 2, d = 3
3. a = 2, b = 3, c = 1
4. a = 1, b= 2, c = 2, d = 2, e = 3

Your score: _____

12–10: Manderstanding. You have it. An understanding of men. You
already know that how they think about sex and how we think
about it is totally different. Nicely done.

9–8: Guy knowledge. You have a bit of it. They are definitely different
than us, but do you know how different? Keep reading and
you'll be surprised.

7–4: Clueless. But don't sweat it. Guys are hard to figure out. They
are so totally different. Who would have thought?

As part of creating your image and determining what's an appropriate level of sexiness, we have to think about your target audience. I'm going to assume, for the purpose of this book, that it's guys. Guys you go to school with. Guys within your age range. Let's say teenage guys.

Now for the tricky part. Your target market is the teenage guy. You want to attract him. You want his attention and ultimately, I will assume, you want him to like you and maybe even date you. He's the reason for any hint of sexiness you might be showing. He's the pot of gold at the end of the rainbow. Don't get all feminazi on me now and start saying you aren't looking for a guy, because if you picked up this book, then you must be concerned about your sex appeal, and sex appeal is for one purpose and one purpose only: to get guys. But if you aren't about the guys and you don't want to date till you're like 30, hold on. You might just need to hear all the same stuff.

DEAR HAYLEY, I don't want to dress sexy. I want to be cute, but I don't want guys drooling all over me. But shopping for clothes that aren't too sexy isn't easy. All the tops are too short and the pants are too low. What can you do? There's nothing out there to wear but sexy stuff. That's why everyone does it. Alyssa

DEAR ALYSSA, Believe me, I know how hard it is to find cute stuff that isn't totally revealing. But it can be done. Trust me. It just takes extra work and some creativity. Layering is a great way to cover up. Also go up a size or two till you find a tee that's long enough. You could just give up and say it's not possible, but that would be a lie. It is possible; you just have to work at it and not compromise when it comes to your fashion. Hayley

I know there can be more to this than just wanting to attract guys. The truth is that most of us girls just want to be cute. We want guys to think we're cute; we want other girls to think we're cute. We just want to feel cute. You can't walk through the mall anymore and feel good about yourself unless you look like the models in the windows. And so you load up on all the latest fashion. For some of us the worst thing can be to not fit in, to not dress like the rest of the world. Believe me, I know. The trouble is that you then become a slave of the fashion world, wearing whatever they design just because it's all there is.

See, the fact of the matter is, regardless of how cute you just want to be or who you want to attract or not attract, all (straight) guys are attracted by different parts of your body that you may or may not have exposed. They aren't all sex crazed—well, maybe they are, but it's natural to some extent. I mean, they have these things called hormones, which do somewhat color how guys see the world, and by that I mean your body. So whether you are targeting them or not, they are looking, and they are assuming that what you're showing them is on the menu you have laid out for them.

THE EYES HAVE IT

Trust me when I say that: guys are visual creatures. They are turned on by what they see. You show them a bit of your boob or some of that long leg of yours and *bam!*—Testosterone City! They are instantly dreaming of what they saw. It might seem gross, juvenile, or impossible that a guy would want to touch your breast just because he can see a part of it, but trust me, it's true. I've talked to hundreds of guys about girls, and it's the same whatever state, country, or province I'm in. They are turned on by your flesh.

We girls are so used to our flesh that we don't think anything about it. We undress in front of each other, we share a dressing room, we sleep together in our T-shirts, and we think nothing of sexual stuff. And so it can seem so strange to us that guys see a little flesh and they go all sexual on us, but it's true. That's why guys are more likely to *not* share a bed, king size or not, with another guy when crashing at a friend's house or on a road trip. *Way too visual for them.* They aren't casual about our bodies like we are. Any hint of flesh they see and it's daydream city, for better or for worse.

So if you are showing the very tippy-top of your cleavage because you think, *Who cares, it's not like they can see my breasts,* funny thing—no, they don't actually see your breasts, but they do start to imagine what they look like.

Their minds start to wander down lower and lower. So show them a whole lot of cleavage and suddenly they're salivating over your entire chest. They can't help but create a mental image of what the rest of you looks like. (Well, they *can* help it, but it's really, really hard. It's instinct, this stuff.) It's the same with your waistline. When you wear your pants down really low on your hips so that your skin shows below your shirt, they are imagining what's down lower. Show them your cute underwear, and it's all over. They're already salivating as if you're wearing nothing from the waist down. This is no joke. Guys' eyes see more than you show them. So the less you are showing, the less they will imagine.

I don't know about you, but I don't like the idea of any ol' guy walking down the hall thinking all fantasy-like on my body and imagining us doing things together. It's kinda gross. Sure, you might feel good about your target guy drooling you up, but he's not the only one in the hall with testosterone, is he? And besides, the Bible makes it pretty clear that causing someone else to stumble (i.e., to fantasize about you) is not cool with God:

Be careful, however, that the exercise of your freedom does not become a stumbling block to the weak.

1 Corinthians 8:9 NIV

But I say to you that everyone who looks at a woman with lust for her has already committed adultery with her in his heart.

Matthew 5:28 NASB

It is better not to eat meat or drink wine *or to do anything else* that will cause your brother to fall.

Romans 14:21 NIV, *emphasis added*

DEAR HAYLEY, My stomach only shows when I raise my hands. That makes my T-shirt raise up, but other than that, I'm covered. Is it okay if my stomach only shows some of the time? Trying

DEAR TRYING, I call that a peep show. It's a subtle part of sexuality, a hint of it from time to time popping out. And believe me, guys are looking for it. That little bitty peek can get men all excited. So check out your clothes and make sure that when you bend over, your cleavage doesn't suddenly overflow your top and that when you raise your hand, your skin isn't flashing everyone. If you want to be obedient to God's Word, then take your body seriously. Even a little glance can lead a guy astray. Hayley

Now that you know that your aggressive exposure of your fleshly parts is a stumbling block to the guys around you, what excuse do you have for flaunting your girly parts? It's really crucial to get this. It's a huge part of your image. Are you claiming to be a believer? Do you worship God, talk about prayer and your relationship to Christ, and then tempt every guy who comes across your path? If we want to develop the perfect image for you, we really have to figure out what that image should be, according to your faith, and then how to achieve it. So this chapter has just been an exercise in understanding the male part of the species that populates this planet with us so that you can better portray the girl that God has designed you to be.

REMEMBERING THE "UNDER" IN "UNDERWEAR"

Ever think it's a cute and sexy little trick to lift the top of your underwear ever so slightly above your waistband? Or what if your undies just happen to show when you sit down? That isn't so bad, is it? I mean, it's not that sexual, is it? Look at it from the guy's perspective. When you show off your underwear, the first thing a guy thinks about is what you look like with just your undies on, and the second thing he thinks is that if you are so willing to show him *part* of your underwear, then you're probably willing to show him *all* of your underwear. In his mind you immediately become, well, sexual—and he will treat you accordingly, which means he will show you attention, but it's purely sexual. That's not to mention all the guys that you don't even know are using you as their own personal peep show.

Basing your image or your relationships on pure sexuality is a recipe for disaster. Guys don't take sexual girls seriously. They just don't. They think about using them until their next conquest. They are so clouded by your body parts that they won't see you for the amazing girl that you are. So be careful when you play around with an image that is "free enough" to expose all your delicates. Besides, you probably didn't buy them at "Victoria's Public Knowledge"! It's not wise to use your freedom, or shall I say flaunt your freedom, in front of guys. It might seem like a cheap thrill, but in the spiritual scheme of things it's a trip down a messy road that can lead to spiritual, physical, and emotional destruction.

MYSTERY GIRL

The truth of the matter is that guys are more attracted, long-term, to the girl who is a bit more mysterious. They like a chase. Think of the caveman: his job was to go out and chase down wild things. It's part of who men are; they love a good chase. Things that are a challenge are much more fun than things that are easy. I mean, he'd much rather play a really challenging game of basketball than an easy game of Candy Land. He likes the challenge. He likes the chance that he might lose. He likes the idea that you aren't that easy to get and that should he get you, he'd be doing something that no other guy (or at least not a ton of them) has done. So **every time you make it too easy on him** by showing him how willing and ready you are, **you lose out**. He starts to think of you less and less as a potential girl-friend and more and more as a great hookup or onetime make-out session.

The key to understanding what guys are thinking is to understand their competitive, adventure-seeking side. Make the pursuit of you more difficult and watch him melt at your feet.

"Talking
to the girls
in my group is
the most difficult
part of my job."

—Confessions of a Youth Pastor

chapter 3

IS YOUR CLOSET Too Hot?

You are what you wear.

Now that you can start to see how guys are totally visual, the next thing to think about is who all is copping a visual on you. This can get really creepy, so hold on. Teenage guys aren't the only ones who have those masculine hormones raging in their loins. It's guys, men, of all ages. From the 22-year-old clerk at the checkout line to the 43-year-old pastor behind the pulpit, they are all men, and they are all turned on by what they see. So it's like this: if you go out sporting your sexiest top that shows just enough of your voluptuous chest and your totally hip miniskirt ever so slightly revealing your lacey undies placed just above the waistband, don't be surprised when I tell you that not only is the hottie down the hall checking you out but every guy from 13 to 83 is catching a glimpse, and their mouths are watering. Sure, some of them might try to look away. But it's hard work. And then they have to fight with their minds and those memories of your supple body. That means that if you walk down the street and see a bench lined with 70-year-old men, they are looking at your breasts and smacking their lips. You are every bit as sexy to the old guy as you are to your target guy. And you think that's gross? Just think about the poor pastor who has to stand in front of his congregation all morning and talk about God while trying to avoid seeing your breasts popping out from your baby doll top. A guy is a guy is a guy, and so if what you're showing ain't on the menu, keep it covered up.

"She looked as if she had been poured into her clothes and had forgotten to say 'when.'"[1]

P. G. Wodehouse

Sexy Girl Translation: Wear clothes that fit!

Showing off more than you're willing to give to a guy is what we call false advertising. A girl who shows off her tummy has to understand that guys think that means she's ready and willing for him to run his hands all over it. He's got sex on his mind as soon as he sees that the doorway to her intimate self says "open for business" like that.

Two kinds of girls wear tops that don't quite connect to their pants. One is the girl who wants guys to want her for her hot stomach, belly button ring, or sexy bottom. She's the one who is ready for action. What she's showing *is* on the menu, and she's proud of it. But the other kind of girl—and this is probably most of you—is the girl who doesn't realize what her sexy tummy is doing to every man that she sees. She doesn't realize that the tummy is the doorway to, well, the parts guys are longing to see and touch. She thinks it's just the style. "I look cute, and who does it hurt?"

Hmm, let me answer that: It hurts the guy who thinks he might get something from you because of what you've got on the menu but then finds out when you reject him that you're just a tease. It hurts the Christian guy who wants to honor God with his thoughts but can't quit thinking about your body. And it hurts you when you suddenly sink to the status of "nice stomach" and are overlooked as a beautiful, intelligent, sensitive, and caring human being. It reduces you to a piece of meat on a menu. It becomes all about the body, and nothing else even comes into focus. Face it, this kind of style is causing another person to stumble just because, well, you have "a right to dress however you want to!"

T-shirts that say something across your breasts are meant to draw attention to them. You don't have to be revealing flesh to get guys to think about your flesh. Be careful what you display across your breasts; you might just be getting the wrong kind of attention.

If you have something written anywhere, it's so people will look. Words written on your bum are very sexy and get guys to think all kinds of things. It's like an offer to open the package. Don't put advertising somewhere unless that's what you're advertising.

A lot of girls get mad when guys treat them too sexually. When guys call them names, or make rude advances, or say nasty stuff to them, they get all in a huff. "How could he talk to me like that? What does he think I am, a piece of meat?" And the answer is *yes*. That's exactly what he thinks you are because that's how you've marketed yourself. The sign in front of your establishment screams "sex." The banner on your ad yells "use me." Guys' eyes become clouded by the flesh, and they lose all sight of the girl inside that flesh. So if you show off parts of you that turn guys on, don't be all upset when they treat you like a sex object. Don't blame them for your PR campaign. You designed it and created the image you wanted to sell to the world, and they're just hoping to get a chance to purchase or steal a piece of you.

Revenue generated by sales
of thongs to 7- to 12-year-old girls
in 2000: $400,000

Revenue generated by sales
of thongs to 7- to 12-year-old girls
in 2002: $1.6 million

Revenue generated by sales
of thongs to 13- to 17-year-old girls
in 2002: $152 million

Source: *Time*,
September 29,
2003

We can't get mad at guys for being guys. We can't blame them for following us down the path of objectification when that's the package we've put together. When you create your own PR package, you have to decide how you want to be treated. What parts of yourself do you want to be considered valuable? Do you want to be just another body for him to take advantage of, or do you want to be something more special? All these things have to be considered every time you get dressed in the morning.

Take a look at this example from *Dateable: Are You? Are They?*

Check it. I am walking down the street wearing a policeman's uniform. I have the hat, the shoes, the badge, the whole deal. I'm walking down the street, minding my own business, when someone runs up to me shouting, "Help! I need help! I was just robbed!"

"Hey, lady, I can't help you," I say.

"What do you mean? You're an officer, you have to help."

"Oh, no. I'm not an officer. I just dress this way."

Translation: *I'm not EZ, I just dress that way.*[2]

You are what you wear. We do judge a book by its cover. One of the major ways people figure out who you are and what you're like is by how you dress. So don't lie to yourself. You really are what you wear.

GOD'S TAKE ON THE SITCH

But don't just take my word for it. We have a better source than that, thank God. And he has a lot to say about your sexuality. Let's take a look so we don't get too far off track:

> But among you there <u>must not be even a hint of sexual immorality,</u> or of any kind of impurity, or of greed, because these are improper for God's holy people.
>
> Ephesians 5:3 NIV, emphasis added

"A hint of sexual immorality." Does that ring any bells? Can you think of anything about your wardrobe that might *hint* at sexual immorality? You don't have to *be* sexually immoral; you just have to *hint* at it. Are your shorts super short? Why? Is your top low cut enough to show cleavage? What's your goal? What about your tummy? Have you pierced it? Tattooed it? Or are you just showing off how tight it is? All of these things are to draw the attention of the male so that he will find you sexually attractive. Bam! A *hint* of sexual immorality.

Dang. Bet you didn't see that coming, did you? I know I didn't the first time I got it. I used to think, *Well, fashion is fashion and low-cut, high-cut, short-cut stuff is in. In fact, it's all I can find. So what's a girl to do?* And I gave in. But when I finally figured out what it was doing to guys, that it was giving them a hint—maybe just a small one, but a hint all the same—that I might be up for some sex play, things got more serious. Because God makes it perfectly clear: NO! You can't play with sex that way. You can't hint around about it or slightly suggest that you might be good in bed by hinting, "Look at this great body." Don't deny it. You know it's true. Heck, even though I was a sworn "virgin till I marry," when I was in school I still found it exciting for guys to think that

I was sexy. I still wanted them to want me—that is, until I figured out what it all meant to their spiritual lives and to my psyche. I can remember thinking, *I have to look sexy so guys will like me, and then eventually I can pick the one I want to marry.* But in the meantime I confused a lot of guys who thought what I was showing *was* on the menu.

I know how hard it is to resist that cute little mini and how great you look in that tight baby doll tee. I know how hard it is to find clothes that don't false advertise, but I also know it has to be done. God makes it clear, we can't play around with our sexiness. It's a powerful tool that should be used for good, not for fun.

God has a purpose for everything. Even your sexuality. And that purpose is the marriage bed. Any other kind of sex or hinting about sex is out of bounds. In fact, it's sinful. "Now the deeds of the flesh are evident, which are: immorality, impurity, sensuality" (Galatians 5:19). Your sexiness isn't something to be played with or taken lightly. So if what you're showing ain't on the menu, keep it covered up.

"Sometimes I scratch my head and wonder,

'What kind of guy is this girl trying to attract?'"

—Confessions of a Youth Pastor

"If most of us
are ashamed of
shabby clothes, . . .
let us be more
ashamed of
shabby
ideas
and shoddy
philosophies. . . .
It would be
a sad situation
if the wrapper
were better
than the meat
wrapped inside
it."[3]   Albert Einstein

Judging Your Self-Esteem?

What you think about yourself is important. Your thoughts manifest themselves in all kinds of ways: how you walk, how you talk, how you carry yourself. What you think about you is really important. And I know that how you dress has a huge effect on how you feel. I mean, having a bad hair day can totally ruin your day. Walk by a mirror and see yourself in old clothes, and suddenly you feel depressed and ugly. I know how it is. We're all girls, and we all have a tendency to be hard on ourselves, but is self-esteem really where it's at? I mean, can you build your self-esteem by having the cutest clothes on the planet or by looking like a hot rock star?

Self-esteem is a precarious thing. It can go up and down based on the outfit of the day. So maybe you should start thinking about a different kind of esteem. After all, God's Word never tells us that we should esteem ourselves. Instead we should be humble, not thinking too highly of ourselves (see Romans 12:3). The meek, not those with high self-esteem, shall inherit the earth (see Matthew 5:5). Yeah, something tells me that self-esteem isn't where we should put all our eggs. Self-esteem is too hard to keep up. It's too hard to manage.

But what if there were another kind of esteem that was more rock solid, less likely to change with the currents? The way I see it, self-esteem is a weak foundation, and the only real foundation for a good mental outlook and a joyful

> ... the only real
> foundation for a
> good mental outlook
> and a joyful spirit is
> *God-esteem.*

spirit is *God-esteem.* When you put your esteem in him and his plans for you, you are never disappointed. Bad things can be said about you, and you aren't fazed because you are hooked up to the Creator of the universe, and he says different of you. God-esteem definitely has more power than self-esteem.

So if you are planning your wardrobe and your look in an effort to build your self-esteem, to make you feel better about yourself, you might want to rethink that. It's just too fleeting. Just one incident can pull the rug out from under you. But if you can focus your mind on what God wants for you, who he made you to be, and who he is, then you will never slip or fall. Your spirit will soar. When people try to put you down, you won't be affected, because your esteem isn't in whether others accept you. When you have a bad hair day, you will blow it off, because in the grand scheme of things, your hair doesn't matter. Yep, God-esteem is where the power is. Let go of tending your own self-esteem and let God become your focus, and you will find that dressing and getting ready every day will become a whole heck of a lot easier.

"If you could only learn the lesson of absolute self-forgetfulness, it would save you a great deal of trial. Out of self and into Christ are the two essential steps always, and the last cannot be fully taken without the first. For just so far as we dwell in self, we are not dwelling in Christ, and just to that degree, therefore, all goes wrong."

Hannah Whitall Smith

"Maybe your purity pledge should start to include where you shop!"

—Confessions of a Youth Pastor

chapter 4

THE ART OF THE BODY

Tattoos and piercings.

Another thing you have to consider in creating your image is body art. You can do so many things to your body to "improve" it, I guess. Lots of people just can't feel complete without a few more earrings, an eyebrow ring, and a tattoo of their favorite animal. And it's all part of the marketing campaign that tells the world who we are and how we want to be thought of. For the purposes of this book, I'm not going into the ethical value of using the body as a blank canvas. If you feel a need for eyebrow piercings or a nose ring, you'll have to take that up with your parents and any prospective employer that might have a hard time hiring someone with metal all over his or her face. Some people can handle it; others can't. But what I am going to talk about is piercings and tattoos that are sexual in nature.

Yes, some body art is created for sexual arousal, not just fashion. The **belly button ring**, for example. It isn't just the latest fashion statement; it's a sexual statement. It's like this: Remember how what you're showing immediately goes onto a menu that guys feel they can now choose from? Okay, have you ever been to a restaurant where they put little icons by their best-selling items so they can get your attention with the best of the best? Well, getting a belly button ring or a **tattoo in the small of your back** just above your pant line is like putting up a sign for the special of the day. It lets everyone know that this area is your featured best seller. In your marketing campaign it's the one thing you want

DEAR HAYLEY, I really want to get a belly button ring. Lots of my friends have them, and I just think they are really cute. What do you think about belly button rings? Curious

DEAR CURIOUS, Belly button rings are cute, I agree. They are not only cute but they are sexy. My one question for you is, what is your goal in wanting one? To show it off? I mean, really, why get one if you aren't going to show it off? But the trouble with that is, it gets guys all excited. A belly button ring is a sexual decoration, plain and simple. You might say, "I'm not going to show it. I'll just know it's there." To that I say, but I bet you're going to tell people about it. And that's almost as bad as showing it. It's a tummy tease. You don't need a belly button ring unless you want to make your stomach more sexy. And sexy stomachs drive men crazy. So it's up to you. What's your goal? And who do you want to be? Hayley

the world to know about you. I know, to you it just looks cute and cool and oh so hip, but to the rest of the world it's just a featured item symbol. Those sexual kinds of body art were created expressly to sell the sexuality of the area where they are placed.

The **tongue ring** is a blatant example of the sexual body art piece. When a guy sees your tongue ring flashing from between your teeth, he's imagining how amazing it will feel on his body. If that's not what you got it for, then you might be totally grossing out right now, 'cuz that's exactly what it's for. And if you knew about this little nugget of information before you got your tongue ring and you got one anyway, you're either a tease or a sexual girl. If this is you, don't expect your romantic dreams to come true. Don't expect guys the world over to be so excited that they all want to shower you with gifts of affection and battle for your undying love. To make yourself a sexual object is to kill a part of you that was created expressly for relationship. God didn't create you to be some boy's toy. He didn't create you to meet the sexual needs of random guys. He made you to be a girl with purpose, someone who will change the world for good just because she lives in it. He made you for one man and one man only, and that man won't be too happy to know that you shared yourself with other men just to get the feeling of being loved.

Here's how God's Word puts it: "Do not conform any longer to the pattern of this world, but be transformed by the renewing of your mind. Then you will be able to test and approve what God's will is—his good, pleasing and perfect will" (Romans 12:2 NIV). So change. Get over what the world says you were created for (the sexual fulfillment of guys) and start to explore what God says you were created for—much, much, much more than that! "'For I know the plans I have for you,' declares the Lord, 'plans to prosper you and not to harm you, plans to give you hope and a future'" (Jeremiah 29:11 NIV).

Neither the American nor the Canadian Red Cross will accept blood donations from anyone who has gotten a body piercing or tattoo in the past year because both procedures can transmit dangerous blood-borne diseases.[4]

"My wife
just started a girls' group
to help them look at the way they dress.
She calls it 'The Navel Academy.'"

—Confessions of a Youth Pastor

All right, I've had my rant. I'm done harping on the little hottie who wants to sexually excite every guy she sees. I want to get back to the average girl, the one who didn't mean to turn on every guy she encounters. The girl who really wants to be obedient and follow the commands of God. I want to get back to the believer who knows God's Word to be true but just didn't know how it applied to everyday things like body art. If you have pierced or tattooed and are starting to feel convicted, don't let the enemy take you down. What you did before you knew the truth is forgiven. It's over. It's water under the bridge. The only thing you have to do now is to repent—that is, to change. To go in a different direction. If you have a sexy tattoo, keep it covered up. Don't flaunt it anymore. If you have a belly button ring, take it out. The only reason you need it is to solicit the sexual attention of guys. And if you don't want to be about that anymore, then be done with it. I don't know how to put it any more clearly. Any piercing or tattoo that is strategically placed on a sexual part of your body achieves only one thing: it gets sexual attention. If you want to change your image, then get rid of the old ways. Become a new person.

Therefore, if anyone is in Christ, he is a new creation; the old has gone, the new has come!

2 Corinthians 5:17 NIV

chapter 5

THE ART OF THE FACE

Makeup, friend or foe?

No discussion of your image would be complete without addressing the idea of face paint, or as we call it nowadays, makeup, the stuff we use to make our faces look beautiful and radiant. Makeup has been around for centuries. The ancient Egyptians were masters of painting their faces as early as 3500 BC. Their reasons varied from the traditional trying to look good to the opposite sex to seeking spiritual protection. They believed that the dark lines they wore around their eyes had magical powers that would protect them from evil spirits. Persians believed henna dyes, used to stain hair and faces, enabled them to summon the majesty of the earth. And in India, henna was thought to contain something of the essence of Lakshmi, the goddess of beauty.

In more recent history, makeup was used to lure the opposite sex. The goal was to make your face look sexually alluring. If you think about what happens when a person gets sexually excited, the correlation between makeup and sexual attraction is easy to see. When we are attracted to someone and become heated with excitement, the blood rushes to our face, like rouge. And our lips get a little bigger—think Botox. Eye shadow draws attention to our eyes and helps us look sexier. Foundation evens out our skin and just makes us look healthier.

Speaking from a strictly instinctual standpoint, we could say that guys choose healthy-looking women because they seem to be the best candidates for bearing healthy children. It doesn't take long to figure out that makeup has a decidedly sexual appeal to it.

In the Middle Ages women stuck adhesive fabrics on their faces. According to FactMonster.com, "**Beauty patches worn on the skin had meaning.** Adhesive fabrics cut in the shapes of stars, hearts, and crosses were worn in the following manner: one to the right of the mouth meant the woman was flirtatious; one on the right cheek meant she was married; one on the left cheek meant she was engaged; and at the corner of an eye meant she was passionate."

Source: http://www.factmonster.com/ipka/A0767816.html

Now, I'm not bashing makeup; I wear makeup. But what I want you to consider is the amount, the colors, and the kind of makeup that you wear. Your face is the first thing that helps people determine who you are and how to react to you. In order to create your best image, we have to take a serious look at your face and how you decorate it. This isn't just a discussion of how, however—it's also a discussion of why. What are your motives, your goals? What do you want to accomplish with your face paint? Just like you have to ask yourself some questions about clothing, you need to ask yourself about your makeup. Are you going for the hot, turned-on sex kitten look, or something a little more subtle?

We usually wear makeup for one of two reasons. One is to look healthier, maybe cover up zits and dark circles, and to just feel better. The other is to look older, which in turn makes you look sexier. Think JonBenet Ramsey, the little beauty queen who was brutally killed. In her pictures she looked like a miniature adult—so much so that she turned on some grown men, who created shrines to her and watched every pageant she was in. What mothers and young girls alike don't understand is that too much makeup too soon can make you look so much older that creepy older guys start getting really turned on. So be aware of your motives. Who are you trying to attract, and what are you doing with your makeup?

"Worldwide cosmetic sales totaled $65 billion annually in 2001."

Encyclopedia Britannica, 2001

Just like your clothes, your makeup reveals to guys what kind of a girl you are. And the truth is, the more makeup, the more sex the guy thinks he's going to get, or at least the more he'll fantasize about—again, because older girls are usually more sexually experienced than younger ones. It isn't even a subliminal thing anymore. A girl with thick black eyeliner and bright red lips speaks volumes to everyone around her. Guys are thinking, *She's ready for anything.* She's got the sign out in front of the shop, saying "open for business and accepting new clients." Tons of makeup is an invitation to guys of all ages to come onto you. Whereas a little less makeup, let's say, the natural look, can just give you an allover healthy glow without screaming "older and more experienced."

Some overly zealous people might say that makeup is altogether evil. They try to tell us that it's for harlots and unacceptable for good Christian girls, but I can't find any references in Scripture to that effect. Some passages do tell us to be careful about how we dress and adorn ourselves, though. That means don't overdo it. The apostle Paul puts it like this: "Likewise, I want women to adorn themselves with proper clothing, modestly and discreetly, not with braided hair and gold or pearls or costly garments, but rather by means of good works, as is proper for women making a claim to godliness" (1 Timothy 2:9–10). In fact, Peter also tells us to *not only* decorate our outside but also our inside: "Your adornment *must not be merely external*—braiding the hair, and wearing gold jewelry, or putting on dresses; but let it be the hidden person of the heart, with the imperishable quality of a gentle and quiet spirit, which is precious in the sight of God" (1 Peter 3:3–4, emphasis added).

Certainly women throughout history have used makeup to allure men, but today using makeup in moderation has become the standard, not something that sets bad girls apart from "good girls." That isn't a license for overdoing it. Like I said before, tons of makeup is a sure signal to guys that you are sexually active. So before you put on your face tomorrow, think about what you want people to think about you. If you want to be considered healthy, clean, and put together, but not overly sexual, then think about cutting back on the heavy stuff and go *au natural* with a little mascara, light blush, and a light lipstick.

The very first hair dryers were vacuum cleaners adapted for drying hair. Alexandre Godefoy invented the first electric hair dryer in 1890.

How Young Is Too Young for Makeup?

The age that you start wearing makeup is between you and your parents. Whatever they say goes! There are no hard and fast rules about the age appropriateness of makeup, but I would say that before high school, you don't need makeup. You still look healthy and clean enough and your skin isn't breaking out. You don't need makeup.

"An estimated 1,282 tubes of lipstick and 2,055 jars of skin care products are sold every minute."

Source: "Beauty in the Mind and Wallet of Beholder," *Minnesota Daily Online*, March 7, 2001

PLASTIC SURGERY

In the past few years, permanent makeup, or plastic surgery, has become all the rage. MTV has a show about kids who want to look like their favorite star and so undergo surgery to change their appearance. And 79,501 teens under 18 got plastic surgery in 2001. Why all the rush to change? Are there really so many horribly disfigured people who have to change in order to survive? The answer is no. For most of these kids, plastic surgery is for "self-improvement," often of the sexual kind. In 2001 the number of girls under 18 who reshaped their noses to make themselves prettier was 29,700.[5]

But, dear ones, nothing could be further from God's heart. Remember, he created each of us just the way we are.

There is a reason for our big nose or floppy ears. They aren't hideous things that have to be corrected; they are beautiful things that make you unique. Our job is to find beauty in ourselves. To believe that it's really what's inside that shines out through all the odd-shaped parts and makes us special. The star of the all-time best-ever movie *Dirty Dancing* had what she considered a large nose. She got it "fixed," and her career went down the tubes. The fixing she did only made her look like everyone else and took away the distinct look her slightly larger nose gave her. If God doesn't want us to be obsessed about decorating ourselves, then he surely doesn't want us to obsess about reconstructing ourselves.

Liposuction: The Easy Way Out

In 2004 3,250 girls under the age of 18 got liposuction.[6] They took the easy way out. God is never one for advocating the easy way out. He tells us that the trials are what make us. We are to consider it pure joy, in fact, when we face trials (see the verse below). And if diet and exercise isn't a trial, I don't know what is! If you are considering liposuction, think about it from a spiritual perspective. What will make you stronger? What will draw you closer to God—a little suction or a whole lot of work?

> Consider it all joy, my brethren, when you encounter various trials, knowing that the testing of your faith produces endurance. And let endurance have its perfect result, so that you may be perfect and complete, lacking in nothing.
>
> James 1:2-4

We are like the butterfly struggling to get out of his cocoon. Taking the easy way out of things by opting for surgery is like cutting open the cocoon to make it easier for the little guy to get out. Trouble is that the butterfly has to struggle and pull at his cocoon in order to build up his wings to be able to fly. Without the struggle, his wings are withered and useless, and he soon dies. The struggle is the good stuff. It's what makes us strong, faithful, and holy. Don't give up on the struggle just because everyone else is. Give God's Word a chance to be proven true.

Don't let your exterior become your obsession or the cost could prove to be your interior
life. Focus on what really matters, your spirit,
your soul, your life with God, and I promise you
that all the exterior stuff will slowly become less
and less important.

The American Society of Plastic Surgeons
reports that over **1.3 million**
people had cosmetic surgery
in the year 2000, and 1.2 million were
women.

Source: American Society of Plastic Surgeons,
http://www.plasticsurgery.org/public_education/
2000statistics.cfm

"I have deeply struggled with my thought life over scantily clad girls in my group."

—Confessions of a Youth Pastor

chapter 6

Birds of a feather flock together.

Another important part of designing the perfect PR campaign for yourself is understanding that people decide a lot about you when they see who you hang out with. Like it or not, people decide a lot about you when they look at your friends. It's not a cliché for no reason that "birds of a feather flock together." It just means that everyone figures you are the same as whom you hang out with. So if your friend is a mean girl, then you are considered a mean girl just by association. Or if she's easy, then you're considered just as easy as she is because she's your bud.

The Bible has something to say about this too. It makes it clear that people don't hang out together unless they are alike or, as the New King James Version puts it, unless they agree. It goes like this: "Can two walk together, unless they are agreed?" (Amos 3:3 NKJV). When you hang out with someone, you endorse who they are and what they do. It's human nature. So if the goal of your PR campaign is to be pure and holy but your best friend has a nasty mouth and loves the boys, then you need to rethink either your campaign or your friendship. Ouch! I know, how could I tell you to ditch your best friend? Listen, it's not about how bad she is but about who you want to be. Your image isn't only important to you; it's important to God. He tells us:

> I wrote to you in my epistle not to keep company with sexually immoral people. Yet I certainly did not mean with the sexually immoral people of this world, or with the covetous, or extortioners, or idolaters, since then you would need to go out of the world. But now I have written to you not to keep company with anyone named a brother, who is sexually immoral, or covetous, or an idolater, or a reviler, or a drunkard, or an extortioner—not even to eat with such a person.
>
> 1 Corinthians 5:9–11 NKJV

The big message in this verse is that if your friend calls herself a believer and doesn't act like one, then you definitely shouldn't be hanging out with her. What does it say about your faith if your entourage is filled with false believers, or lukewarm ones at best? According to this verse, you can't allow it any longer. You are who you hang out with. And so if she calls herself a believer and is being sexually immoral, partying, drinking, or making idols for herself of her clothes, her money, her car, or anything else, you can't be her best friend anymore, or you are no better than her.

God's ultimate message on this subject is, "Do not be deceived: 'Evil company corrupts good habits'" (1 Corinthians 15:33 NKJV). See, God knows that we become like who we hang out with and we also make others think we already are like those we hang out with. If your believing friend isn't being faithful, she is bringing you and your God down.

This is serious business; it isn't as easy as just saying, "Oh well, she'll get better." She might get better, but it might take you telling her that you can't hang out with her anymore for her to do it. Don't let her put a guilt trip on you and tell you, "You just think you're better than me." That's not it at all. You just think your God demands more sanctification of you. More setting apart. He isn't pleased with the actions you've allowed in your life, so you need to distance yourself from them. I know this sounds like such an extreme thing to do, but if your faith isn't extreme, then what good is it? Part of being faithful involves pain. It hurts when we separate from the world.

If your friend is not a Christian, the story is a bit different. You can't go around avoiding every sinner in the world, because you are in the world to save sinners. You can't just dump her because she's living in sin; that's what nonbelievers do—they live in sin. But you can't spend all your time with her, either. She can't be your best friend because she's not in agreement with you on faith. The truth is that she can never share in the deepest part of your heart. She can't understand your choices, your actions, your hopes, your motivations, or your dreams, because they are all based on your faith, something she thinks is nonsense. The Bible says, "Do not be unequally yoked together with unbelievers. For what fellowship has righteousness with lawlessness? And what communion has light with darkness?" (2 Corinthians 6:14 NKJV). The truth of this word is that you can't have communion with darkness. You can't be best friends with nonbelievers because that supposes some kind of agreement, and obviously when it comes to the most important thing in the world—faith in God—you don't agree. She will never truly understand you because of who you are: a believer in Christ Jesus.

I know this seems like a hard one to swallow. And it is. But if you want to be real in your faith and real with your God, then you have to consider all of his Word and not just the parts that make your life easier. When your best friend is a wild, partying, sexual nonbeliever, your image, who the world thinks you are, is tainted. They associate you with your friend, and if she is living life large as a wild girl, then you look like just as wild of a girl.

When it comes to cutting back on seeing your best friend, don't expect her, the nonbe-

A friend is defined as "one attached to another by affection or esteem." Consider if you are attached to the right kind of people.

liever, to get it. She won't. God's Word makes that clear: "For the message of the cross is foolishness to those who are perishing, but to us who are being saved it is the power of God. . . . Where is the wise? Where is the scribe? Where is the disputer of this age? Has not God made foolish the wisdom of this world?" (1 Corinthians 1:18, 20 NKJV). What God demands of us seems like pure folly to the world. They don't get it, and they won't get it until they make him Lord of their lives as well. But until then, you've gotta do what you've gotta do. You have to work on your own sanctification. You have to be set apart. You can no longer plead ignorance on this topic. Bad company corrupts good character. Don't let your loose, immoral, or apathetic friend corrupt your character in the eyes of the world or of God.

What I'm hoping right now is that your desire for the perfect image is in sync with God's plan for your life. He wants you to be sanctified—that is, set apart from the rest of the world. Not isolated and shut off from it but different from it. Throughout the Bible, God's people continued to mix with people who rejected God, people he told them not to blend with, and repeatedly, when they did, they were punished for it. God isn't trying to cut us off from the world; he's just trying to keep us pure. We can't be pure if we give our hearts to the children of the enemy—that is, if we become best friends with them.

So what does all this mean? It doesn't mean that you have to avoid all nonbelievers; it just means you need to make some effort to make friends with believers who will hold you up and help you be sanctified. Surround yourself with strong believers who will help you become who you want to be, both internally and externally. Don't cut yourself off from the world and your nonbelieving friends; just find some more believers to add some salt and light to the mix. And if your friend is just the wrong girl for you—say she's too wild or too loose—then you might need to consider cutting things off altogether, because you don't want her to lead you down that same path of destruction. You're smart enough to figure this out. Use your head. Don't become a zealot or anything; just consider your friends, what role they play in your life, and what God's Word has to say about it. Avoid immoral believers, and temper your moral nonbeliever friends with strong believers added in. You can do this, and when you do, your new PR package will shine just like you want it to.

"If you're

showing skin

regularly,

ask yourself,

'Who are my

fashion

role models?'

and,

'Are they living

a worthy

and holy

life?'"

—Confessions
   of a Youth Pastor

chapter 7

THE TEASE

Could you be one?

tease:

to tantalize
especially
by arousing
desire or
curiosity
without
intending to
satisfy it[7]

"You are such a tease!" Have you ever heard those words? I sure have. All through high school I was called a tease. And I never understood it till I got much older. I mean, what could I do? How could I help it if guys wanted me and I was unattainable? I was committed to abstinence. But was I really? Or, did I really undermine my own commitment by leading guys on in their minds? The truth is that the tease, though oftentimes completely oblivious, is really leading guys down a path of sexual sin without doing much of anything at all.

The tease is a tease because she tantalizes the sexual appetite of guys, either consciously or subconsciously. If you are being called a tease, I'll assume for the purposes of this chapter that it's because you are oblivious to what your body is doing to the guys and men around you. So let's talk about what your body is doing to guys.

The tease can lead guys on with her body and with her words. I was a big flirt in school. I had such a quick tongue that it was effortless, and even fun, for me to flirt with all the guys. The trouble was that I didn't realize what my taunting was doing to them. I guess I just didn't see the extent to which guys are slaves to their sexual desires. They are easily turned on and easily aroused, so that even words can get them going. I'm not saying that flirting is altogether evil, but I am saying that you have to be careful not to let it get too overboard, especially when it's with a guy you aren't interested in at all. Flirting is reserved for giving the guy you like clues that it's okay to ask you out, not for making sexual advances. Don't use it to get guys all hot and bothered and then walk away from them. Watch how you use your words, my little flirt. If you can keep up with the witty banter and sexual innuendo of the guys, beware. This makes you a tease—unless, of course, you're following through with your nasty talk, but I sure hope you're not.

The tease is also dangerous for the spiritual lives of guys because of the way she dresses. I've already talked about the idea that if what you're showing ain't on the menu, you need to keep it covered up. Now, I don't want to beat a dead horse . . . but if what you're showing ain't on the menu, keep it covered up! You become a tease, playing with the sexual appetites of guys, when you give them a peak at your cleavage, your stomach, or too much leg, to put it bluntly. When you let a guy see the parts of you reserved for the sexual side of you, you tease him to no end. His hormones start racing, and the tease is complete. All you have to do is say something like, "Eww, gross!" and walk away, and you've left a guy in misery. It's just not cool to give guys a peek at your privates. It's not cool to think, "Oh, I'm not hurting anyone by showing this part of my skin. No one even notices." Lies! They do notice, and teasing isn't funny! It isn't fair. It's like playing the devil, leading every guy in your path down the path of destruction. As Jesus himself put it, "But whoever causes one of these ~~little ones~~ guys who believe in Me to stumble, it would be better for him to have a heavy millstone hung around his neck, and to be drowned in the depth of the sea. Woe to the world because of its stumbling blocks! For it is inevitable that stumbling blocks come; but **woe** to that ~~man~~ girl through whom the stumbling block comes!" (Matthew 18:6–7, emphasis added).

We can't mess around with the spirits and hearts of those around us. It just isn't holy, and it most certainly isn't safe. Jesus makes it pretty clear that to do so carries a terrible price. He says "woe" to those who are the stumbling block—in this case, the tease. And in case you aren't sure what "woe" is, let me give you the def:

woe: a condition of **deep suffering** from misfortune, affliction, or grief; **ruinous trouble**[8]

Woe! Not a thing you want to play around with. Before you read this, you had the excuse of ignorance. You don't have to worry about being in deep spiritual trouble, because you didn't know what you were doing, and God judges your heart and your motives. He knows you didn't get it till now. But now that you do get it, the rules have changed. Now you are responsible for how you dress. It's up to you not to tease the guys around you. You can no longer make yourself a stumbling block to the men in your path. If you do, woe to you!

As you're reading this book, several times you might have wanted to just rip open your closet and get rid of half your clothes so you'll never mess up again. Lots of girls are doing that, and it can be a freeing experience that creates a fresh start. But what you might want to do instead is get one of your friends a copy of this book too. Let her read through it and then,

DEAR HAYLEY, How far is too far when it comes to cleavage? What if they can see just the top part? Is that bad? Kayla

DEAR KAYLA, Cleavage is really hard to cover up. Most tops show off some of it. But the truth is that even a little bit of cleavage can get guys hot. They start imagining what the rest of you looks like, and *bam!*— it's fantasy city. I think the best rule of thumb is, don't let them see the start of your cleavage, even when you bend over. That's a total peep show. So check yourself in the mirror or ask your friend what she sees when you bend over. Guys love breasts, and they are always looking to see what can be seen. Cover up as best you can so they don't get a peep show when you bend over. Hayley

at the final chapter, "Dressing Party," you two can go through your clothes together, maybe even with an adult or big sis, and talk about what's off limits and what's good for your new PR campaign.

I call being a tease fake modesty, and that might need a little explanation. It's like this: modesty is all the rage in the Christian church. Everyone is signing abstinence pledges and promising to wait till marriage. But to wait for what? For sex, sure, but what about all that other stuff that goes along with it, like the teasing? You can be totally sold out on abstinence and still be leading guys to sin sexually. So the tease is really faking her modesty. She is speaking modesty with her lips, but then her actions say the complete opposite. Modesty isn't just agreeing that sex is wrong; it's agreeing that guys are visual creatures and that you have a huge responsibility in protecting them from your body. You can't claim to be modest and be showing guys certain parts of your body. It just doesn't work that way. So the tease needs to come to terms with her body and her talk and then make an agreement with herself and God that she will no longer be a stumbling block to the guys that see her.

You act the way you dress.

Think about it.

Gross Guy Note

If you still don't buy the whole teasing thing, then think about it like this. It's really gross, but it has to be said: when you are a tease (or you just dress like one), every guy who sees you has a chance to make a movie of you in his mind— a movie rated anything he wants, like PG-13, R, or even XX.

When you show off too much of yourself and creepy guys see you, I guarantee that they are taking you home with them in their minds. And I don't know about you, but I don't want to be the star in some guy's nightly fantasy. Eww!

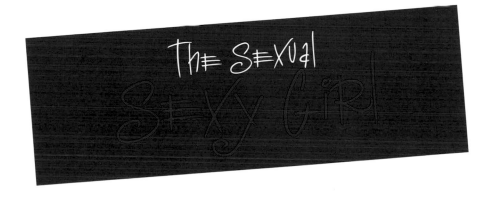

chapter 8

The Sexual Sexy Girl

What's sex got to do with it?

The big question that everyone wants to ask is, *How far is too far physically?* How far can I go and still be "pure"? It's a good question, one that would be good to figure out as we develop a new PR image for you. Because what you do is just as important as how you look in conveying to the world who you are and how you should be treated.

Over the past decade a lot of students have signed some kind of abstinence pledge, promising to stay pure until the day of their wedding. But the truth is that a lot of you signed the pledge because everyone else did too. I mean, what were you going to do, refuse to sign it and have everyone think you're pro sex and anti-abstinence? So you went to the front of the room and made your pledge. You agreed to abstain from sex until marriage. And then the cute guy comes calling, or your guy friend wants to fool around just because you're friends and why not, it's not *exactly* sex. . . . The truth is that the abstinence pledge has done nothing to eliminate the sex play and sexually transmitted diseases that plague your generation. Before you say, "Oh, not me. I'm not guilty of anything. I'm totally sex free; I haven't done anything against my pledge," take a look at these sex games that might just be more sex than you bargained for.

FRIENDS WITH BENEFITS

It seems to be all the rage right now: "friends with benefits." You're such good friends, and so you totally trust each other. You spend all this time together, and neither of you has a significant other, so why not share a few innocent kisses or a mild make-out session? Who is it hurting? The answer is that it's hurting you. It's hurting your image, because now you look easy. You don't need love to make out. You're officially a plaything. And it's hurting—no, *staining*—your purity. When you allow a friends-with-benefits relationship into your life, you lose a valuable part of you. You give away a little bit of yourself every time you fool around with a guy.

I know it seems like an emotionally safe choice, but the truth is that one of the two in the relationship always ends up feeling more than the other, and in the end the friendship suffers, as does the one who feels the most. It's not a "no strings attached" relationship. As soon as the physical comes into it, there are strings. When one of the two of you gets a significant other, what happens then? Do the make-out sessions stop? Do you still hang out, minus the kissing? How do you think your boyfriend will feel if he finds out you've been fooling around with your best friend?

Face it, friends with benefits is a big lie. It's one of satanic proportions. That means it's straight from the devil's mouth. He's convinced you that your body and your sexuality are just for fun; they have no real significant spiritual purpose, so why not use them to your advantage? In the process he is destroying friendships and making it easier and easier for you to go farther and farther sexually, because you feel "safe." And he's doing all he can to subvert God's law, which makes it clear that you are to abstain from sexual immorality, and that means anything that gives a hint of sexual immorality. Making out with a "friend" is devaluing your body and

yourself. It's making a game of something that is very special to your God. So don't think that friends with benefits is your answer to your sexual frustration. It really is just the beginning.

As many as 70% of college students admit to having engaged in sexual activity primarily as a result of being under the influence of alcohol, or to having sex they wouldn't have had if they had been sober.[9]

Some facts about alcohol and the female body, why we get drunk easier than guys.

- o Women have a smaller quantity of dehydrogenase, an enzyme that breaks down alcohol.
- o Premenstrual hormonal changes cause intoxication to set in faster during the days right before a woman gets her period.
- o Alcohol increases estrogen levels. Birth control pills or other medicine with estrogen increase intoxication.[10]

ALCOHOL AND YOUR SEX LIFE

A lot of good girls go bad when alcohol is involved. Time and time again, girls who wouldn't normally fool around with a guy at a party are suddenly open to it when they drink a little. Alcohol taints the way you see the world. It's another great tool of Satan to get you off track. But it's no excuse for tainting your purity and falling into a make-out or sex session. Some girls plead ignorance or weakness—"I just didn't realize what I was doing"—but that's no excuse. It's still immoral. And it's still a slap in the face of the purity that God calls you to when you liquor up and then let happen what happens. Beware of drinking at parties. Beware of the guys who see this as an invitation to use you up.

When it comes to your PR package, adding drinking to the mix sends all the wrong signals. It lets guys know that what you stand for sober isn't what you stand for drunk and that all bets are off. If you are a believer, they might even look at you as a juicier target because they will think you are untouched, untainted, and they love getting ahold of that. But it isn't what you think. It isn't true love. It isn't romance. It isn't something that could turn into something. It's a guy using you for all you give and then walking away.

HOW FAR IS TOO FAR?

To ultimately answer this question, we have to look at God's law and his words for us when it comes to our sexuality—how we dress and how we act. The guys we attract are ultimately the gage of our sexuality. If we lived in a world of all girls, heck, we could walk around naked and no one would care. But the truth is that guys just can't handle the full force of our sexuality, and as children of God we need to consider what we are doing to others around us. If you want to know how far is too far, think about this verse:

> You have heard that it was said, "You shall not commit adultery"; but I say to you that everyone who looks at a woman with lust for her has already committed adultery with her in his heart.
>
> Matthew 5:27–28

You can't control the minds of the men you encounter, but you can help to alleviate the problems they have when looking at a sexy girl. Think about your wardrobe, the way you dress, and the things you do with your guy friend, and then ask yourself this: "Am I causing him to lust? Is he getting turned on by this?" If so, then you're leading him to sin.

Don't let God's Word fall by the wayside. He is serious when he says that to even look at a girl and *want* to have sex with her is sinful. And he's just as serious when he tells us that things go very badly for people who lead others to sin. Don't allow yourself to be a tool of the enemy and to lead guys down the path of sinfulness. When you are getting dressed, consider how you look to guys. When you are alone with your guy, consider what you are doing to his sex drive, and stop before you get him revved up so much that he is lusting after you.

There are all kinds of ways to interpret "going too far."

And every person seems to have their own idea of how far is too far. But God's Word makes it clear. Now it's up to you. Will you find the loopholes and try to get around God's law or will you take a long hard serious look at your sexual options and consider his thoughts on the matter? Whether it's a system like friends with benefits or the lie of "the alcohol made me do it," be careful which deception of the enemy you believe. If you can be honest with yourself about your sex life and God's thoughts on it, you can create a much stronger PR campaign that will empower you to find the love of your life and not a "this'll do in the meantime" kinda thing. Think it over. What kind of life do you want to live?

chapter 9

The
ANTI-SEXY
Girl

Just one of the guys.

Not all girls are the same. Some of you are probably reading this and saying, "Sexy, who wants to be sexy? I want to be comfortable." You're the girl who likes to wear baggy T-shirts and basketball shorts. You're the girl who could care less for fashion and least of all for being sexy. More than likely you're "one of the guys." You love sports. You don't play all those girly mind games. You aren't about tracking down the next hottie. Although you'd like to have a cute guy by your side, it's not your sole goal in life. Good for you. It's healthy not to be playing the cutie trying to get a guy all the time. But let's talk a bit about who you are: the antisexy girl.

Have you ever noticed that your clothes look a lot like your guy friends' clothes? You probably even like to wear their clothes when you get the chance. And like I said, you are probably one of the guys and wonder why you don't get asked out on too many dates. The answer might be in your chosen PR campaign. Let me just give you a little insight as to what your choice of attire says to the world.

When you dress like you just came off the basketball court, you bring a lot of things to mind: exercise, sweat, aggression . . . things that don't exactly exude femininity. Your form is hidden under the sacklike clothes you feel best in, so guys are not even beginning to think of you as a girl. You have the air of being anything but a girl, really, so that might be why it's harder for you to get a date than other girls. Dressing like a guy or avoiding your femininity sends mixed signals to the male population. Sure, they know you're a girl, but from looking at you they determine that you aren't too happy with that. You'd almost rather be a guy. And who can blame you, right? I mean, girls can be a real pain in the butt. But they aren't supposed to be. They are supposed to be caring and loving, nurturing and giving, sensitive and loving. They are the perfect counterpart for the male psyche. But when you hide that part of you in your rough exterior, you create for yourself a PR plan that says, "I'm not interested in being a girl." And so guys treat you like a buddy.

Now, there's nothing wrong with being comfortable. And it's great that you aren't revealing all your body parts like some other girls. But deciding to wear every day the same clothes you wear to work out or to sleep is a PR choice that definitely taints the way people think about you. Words like sloppy, careless, disinterested, and uncreative come to mind. Can you see a starlet walking around in her volleyball clothes 24/7? Or showing up to work in her pajamas? It just wouldn't fly. Dressing like a guy—really, they wear the exact same workout gear—is telling the world you don't give a darn about your femininity. But the thing is, that femininity is how you were made. You were made a girl. A soft, sweet, yummy girl who has chosen to hide herself in androgynous clothing so as not to be noticed. And there can be some comfort in that. You blend in. No one takes notice of you. But truthfully, is that what you want? Or would you rather be the girl God made you, curves and all? This doesn't mean you should go out and start dressing all sleazy, but it is a call to start thinking about what your choice in apparel says to the rest of the world.

Before you say, "I don't care! I'm happy being a slob. It's just who I am," let's take a little bitty journey into God's Word and see if he has anything to say about the matter. I mean, surely he doesn't care what girls wear . . . or does he?

A woman shall not wear man's clothing, nor shall a man put on a woman's clothing; for whoever does these things is an abomination to the LORD your God.

Deuteronomy 22:5

Now I know this is Old Testament law and we don't follow every rule anymore, but why do you suppose God would bother to mention in the Bible how we should dress? Why would he care enough to let his people know that it's not appropriate for girls to dress like guys and guys to dress like girls? Perhaps it's because he wants us to live up to who we were created to be. Especially in a world with so much sexual confusion, this passage would seem to still be important to the believer's life.

Consider your wardrobe in light of this verse. Do you think that you wear clothes that guys would wear? Do you look like a guy when you walk down the hall? Do you refuse to dress "girly"? I know from experience that dressing girly can make you feel weird. I used to be just like that. I wore big, baggy guy clothes in college when dressing like a boy was in. And it worked for me because I didn't want anyone to notice my body, so I hid it all the time, feeling like it was a sin to be feminine. But this wasn't a healthy desire; I realized later that it came from fear—fear of who I was and who I wasn't. Maybe something in your past makes you afraid to be a girl. Something someone said or did. It's time to start thinking about who you really are and not who you were trained to be. Nothing is wrong with your femininity. I know it feels like a bad thing sometimes. But it is your destiny. You were made a girl for a specific reason, and to deny that is to tell God he got something wrong.

I can just hear you saying, "Wow, that's drawing a lot of conclusions from how I dress." But that's what this whole PR campaign is about. People draw conclusions about other people by the way they dress. Your outfit is your presentation to the rest of the world of who you think you are. Are you a girl unhappy about being a girl? Do you think God got it all wrong? Or are you willing to step up and claim your femininity, even if it seems like a foreign concept right now? Femininity is defined as the quality or nature of the female sex. It is what makes us unique and what makes us girls. It's also what attracts guys to us. If you are at all interested in boys, then think about your clothes. Do they show that you are comfortable being the girl in the relationship? Do they accentuate your femininity, or do they send a mixed message about who you are? The clothes you choose to be seen in every day will tell the world how you feel about yourself and how you want to be treated. Consider what your wardrobe says to the world and if that's who you truly want to be.

Differences between the Sexes

A man has at most 6 items in his bathroom—a toothbrush, toothpaste, shaving cream, razor, a bar of soap, and one towel that hasn't been washed in a month.

The average number of items in a typical woman's bathroom is 437. A man would not be able to identify most of these items.

"Jewelry or body art is trying to attract attention to that area, yet I can get fired for staring at your belly button or the small of your back.

Thanks a lot."

—Confessions of a Youth Pastor

Creating an Image You Love

chapter 10

Join us.

sanctification = a process of ongoing change toward being holy that begins when you accept Christ and never stops.
holy = set apart, distinct; different from the sinful world around you. It means being like God. Wow!

What I've been talking about in terms of our sexuality is really revolutionary. The rest of the world doesn't buy all this new creation, holy obedience mumbo-jumbo. They are strangling themselves one sexual encounter at a time. But what we are talking about here is a major change in character. It's a change in life experiences, a turning toward what is righteous and good. If we keep taking the world's idea of normal or acceptable and allowing into it our spiritual world, we are killing our souls as well as our hearts and minds. God wants you to be sanctified. That's what this book is about at the heart of it. How does a sanctified girl dress, act, look? How is she different? Does she have to be a geek? I think not. Does she have to be odd? No way. But she does have to be *different*. And we can thank God that different is an awesome thing.

Before we go any further, I want to do a quick study on God's plan for your life. That plan is easier to find than you think. It's written in the words of the Bible. It's really not rocket science, it's just biblical truth. God has a plan for you, and he's made it totally clear—you just have to be willing to read. His master plan for your life is your *sanctification*. Big word for a big process that might leave you bruised and aching. It might make you feel like you've been running a marathon or climbing a mountain. It will most definitely leave you feeling different, acting different, and, well, just being different. It's major reconstructive surgery. It's the hardest and the best thing you'll ever do, this sanctification. Let's dive into it a bit before we get back into your image, because this should play a major part in creating your PR plan.

Sanctification—your process of becoming more and more holy—is a thing that is continually happening; it never stops and so it requires a continual exercise of faith. And the good news is, it's not something you do alone. It's something God helps you with every step of the way. It involves prayer, his Word, and even discipline. He helps correct your path by teaching you where the land mines are. He disciplines those he loves so that they can be corrected and moved closer to holiness. God's goal is not to make you happy; it's to make you holy. I know that sounds like a rip-off, but the truth is that those who are holy are in a continual state of joy. They don't get burned by people, because their focus is on God. They don't get used by people, because they live by God's law. They truly have it all. Happiness based on things and other people comes and goes, and that's not God's ultimate goal for you. Remember that sanctification thing? He wants you to be special. He wants you to stand out. He wants you to be different than the rest of the world. And if you're willing to go there with him, he'll do all it takes to get you there.

Let's see what his Word has to say about Sexy Girls. Read these verses and use them to answer the questions below them. That's where we get the truth—from God's Word, not from the world.

> For this is the will of God, that you should be **consecrated** (separated and set apart for pure and holy living): that you should abstain and shrink from all sexual vice, that each one of you should know how to possess (control, manage) his own body in consecration (purity, separated from things profane) and honor, not [to be used] in the passion of lust like the heathen, who are ignorant of the true God and have no knowledge of His will.
>
> 1 Thessalonians 4:3–5 AMP

What is God's will for your life? _____

_____

_____

> Do not offer the parts of your body to sin, as instruments
> of wickedness, but rather offer yourselves to God, as those
> who have been brought from death to life; and offer the parts
> of your body to him as instruments of righteousness.
>
> Romans 6:13 NIV

Now that you've read some of this book and are seeing how God's Word relates to your sex life, what does this mean for what you do with your body? _____

_____

_____

In the next verse underline all the things that have to do with the "sinful mind" and **circle** all the things that have to do with "the mind controlled by the Spirit."

> The mind of sinful man is death, but the mind controlled by
> the Spirit is life and peace; the sinful mind is hostile to God.
> It does not submit to God's law, nor can it do so.
>
> Romans 8:6–7 NIV

Which do you want to be controlled by—the sinful mind, or the Spirit? _____

But Isn't It All about Grace?

A lot of people think that the purpose of God is really grace more than sanctification—that his main goal is to show you grace, to forgive you for all you've done. And so they use that trump card to do whatever they want, because they know they'll be forgiven. But watch out. God's Word is really clear that there is a way to outrage the Spirit of grace. To really tick him off so there's "no grace for you!" Check it out:

> For **if we go on sinning deliberately after receiving the knowledge of the truth, there no longer remains a sacrifice for sins**, but a fearful expectation of judgment, and a fury of fire that will consume the adversaries. Anyone who has set aside the law of Moses dies without mercy on the evidence of two or three witnesses. How much worse punishment, do you think, will be deserved by the one who has **spurned the Son of God**, and has **profaned the blood of the covenant by which he was sanctified**, and has **outraged the Spirit of grace**? For we know him who said, "Vengeance is mine; I will repay." And again, "The Lord will judge his people."
>
> Hebrews 10:26–30 ESV, emphasis added

**Be careful with grace.
Don't abuse it.**
God knows the motives of your heart,
and he knows if you are just having fun
today knowing tomorrow you will ask
for forgiveness.

It doesn't work like that, my dear.

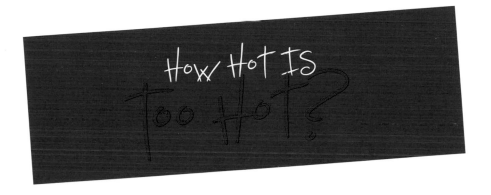

chapter 11

A self-analysis.

You're almost ready to create the perfect PR and publicity package. No more walking out of the house without a plan. No more accidental fashion. Now it's time to study your current self and see how you want to change your marketing and PR package. Let's figure out who you want to be, what you want to look like, and what you want people to think about you, and then let's get to work.

The first thing I want you to do right now is go back to the first chapter, where you answered all those questions about your image and who you want to be. This is your jumping-off point. If you were honest, this is the truth about where your PR presentation should go. All good PR agents know they have to define the talent (i.e., the starlet) before they can design the perfect package for them. So you have to agree with yourself about who you want to be. Go back now and read what you wrote. This is the foundation for your plan.

Go ahead, go back. I'll wait right here.

Now that you've looked over your initial ideas on who you want to be, write a small summary of what you thought about yourself and your image when you started this book.

_____

_____

_____

Okay, now let's take all that stuff a little deeper. Here are a few questions that you need to answer in order to make sure you really agree with yourself and are committed to who you are in Christ and how he wants your PR package to appear to the rest of the world.

Read this verse and think over your life:

You have heard that it was said, "You shall not commit adultery"; but I say to you that everyone who looks at a woman with lust for her has already committed adultery with her in his heart.

Matthew 5:27–28

Are you doing anything that might make a guy, any guy who sees you or touches you, lust for you in his heart and thus commit adultery? Remember that doing so is leading someone else into sin, and Jesus tells us that's one of the worst things we could do. So take some time to think about how you dress and act, and be honest. Are there things you do that might make guys and men lust for you? If so, write them down here so that you can be sure to repent of them:

_____

_____

Likewise, I want women to adorn themselves with proper clothing, **modestly** and **discreetly**, not with braided hair and gold or pearls or costly garments, but rather by means of good works, as is **proper for women making a claim to godliness**.

1 Timothy 2:9–10, emphasis added

What was proper clothing in biblical times and what is proper now are obviously two completely different things. Thinking about what your parents and maybe your pastor might consider proper, how are you doing? Are you underdressing? Showing off a little too much skin here and there? Consider God's Word on how he wants us to dress, and then write down your position on clothes.

How hot is too hot? How much flesh do you think is okay to show, and where do you draw the line?

_____

_____

_____

Before we go any further, let's do a little study. Paul uses the word *modesty* in the verse you just read. What do you think it means? _____

Do you have a desire to be modest? Before you answer that, you might want to think about the definition of modesty. According to Webster's dictionary, *modesty* is "propriety in dress, speech and conduct." And *propriety* is "conformity to what is socially acceptable."

What modesty *isn't* is looking like a nun or an Amish person. Modesty isn't an outdated idea; it's actually in keeping with the times. It means fitting in, not being too far out there. Not shocking people with your clothes and speech. I guarantee you that if you walk into church with a miniskirt and baby doll top on, you are not wearing the right attire for where you are. You are sticking out like a sexual sore thumb. And if you go to the beach all covered from head to toe like a nun, you will stick out as well. Modesty is about looking normal. Not drawing tons of attention to yourself so that you shock people or cause them to stumble. So rethink that weird word modesty, and then consider whether you want to follow Paul's teaching when he tells women (that's you) to dress modestly in keeping with the times.

Do you want to be modest? _____

The second big word Paul uses here is *discreetly*. How do you think you can dress discreetly? Like Catwoman, all in black so you blend in with the night? Or maybe in a gunny sack so no one notices you at all? Nope, none of those are true. Let's check it out:

discreet = having or showing discernment or good judgment

So, being discreet is just being smart. Now that you know that guys are looking if you are showing and that they are fantasizing a lot of the time too, what do you think is good judgment when it comes to your clothes and your actions?

_____

_____

_____

The next thing Paul mentions is braids and jewelry and such:

Likewise, I want women to adorn themselves with proper clothing, modestly and discreetly, **not with braided hair and gold or pearls or costly garments**, but rather by means of good works, as is proper for women making a claim to godliness.

1 Timothy 2:9–10, emphasis added

This isn't the Bible forbidding hairstyles—again, think about what is appropriate for the times. In biblical times braids were not cool, whereas now they are very normal, so this part of the verse is "descriptive" of the times and not a formula for how you should wear your hair or your jewelry. That is key to the final part, which talks about what really makes a woman beautiful. It's her actions, her good works, all the good and holy things she does. That should be your emphasis, much more than your outfit. What

are you doing with your time? How do you treat others? As you consider your PR image, be sure you consider your actions, not just how you dress but how you treat other people and how you live out your holiness.

Now that we've taken a longer journey through this verse, any other thoughts you have about how hot is too hot when it comes to your clothing and your actions?

_____

_____

_____

So how hot is too hot? I think you are

old enough and smart enough to answer that. Having read this book, you know what God wants for you. You have his Word, and that is your guide, not me. I'm just here to get you to think about God's Word and how it relates to your everyday, walking-around life. Hopefully you've done some thinking and you've considered your Creator's words about sexy. Is it okay to be sexy? If you're ready to answer "no" then I hope you've made some adjustments to your thoughts and you are ready to embark on a new, revolutionary PR campaign that will show the world just what you think of your God and his Word.

The next step on this journey is to write a small PR plan that summarizes who you want to be, how you want to look, and what you want to be thought of as. It doesn't have to be too long; it's just a definition that you will want to keep near you so that when it comes time to shop for clothes, pick friends, and figure out what you will do with your life, you'll be totally clear on your choices before they need to be made.

Write a small description of how you want to be seen so that a PR agent could read it and then help you attain that goal. Something like this:

I want people to see me as a smart, kind person who has a fun personality and loves people. I want people to see my happy side, the part of me that makes people laugh and have a good time.

Or

I want people to take me seriously. I want to be seen as the smart girl who has a lot of close friends and treats others with respect and kindness. I want to be respected too for my mind and my heart.

_____

_____

_____

_____

If you can clearly write out who you want others to see when they see you, then it will make it so much easier to become that person. Once you can describe your own PR campaign, it is just that much closer to becoming a reality. You can't go somewhere unless you know where you're going. You wouldn't get in the car and drive around with no destination and then be surprised you never got anywhere. The same is true with life. If you have a goal, a destination then you can get there, but if you have no goal, and you can't articulate your destination in life, then how do you expect to get there? So spend some time on this. Make sure you really are committed to this image and then start heading in that direction.

chapter 12

Are you ready?

Now that you know who you are and how you want to be looked at by God and the rest of the world, it's time to make it real. It's time to let God know you are serious about what you have decided. My hope is that you want to draw closer to him, to be more like his Son, and to dress and act accordingly. After having read all his truth about how important it is to maintain your sexual purity, I'm hoping you are feeling an urge to take a more spiritual approach to your dress and behavior. Walking this road will be challenging. It will be hard to find the right clothes to wear, and people might think you are weird, avoiding sexy, but in the end you will be honored by a God who rewards those who do his will.

The first step in this journey of change is to come clean. All of us have flubbed up. All of us have been ignorant of God's law in some area or another and have messed up because of it. But you have forgiveness if you confess how you messed up when you thought sexy was good for you. God wants a clean slate; he wants a real confession. He wants you to be honest with yourself and with him. So what I want you and your friend(s) to do now is to make a commitment to God to honor his law and his desire for your purity.

CONFESS YOUR SINS

1. Get Real. You can't hide anything from God, so it's time to get real. Call yourself a sinner, admit that your idea of being sexy is wrong, and let's move on.

> If we say that we have no sin, we are deceiving ourselves and the truth is not in us. If we confess our sins, He is faithful and righteous to forgive us our sins and to cleanse us from all unrighteousness. If we say that we have not sinned, we make Him a liar and His word is not in us.
>
> 1 John 1:8–10

2. Tell Someone. For some reason confession becomes more real when you have to admit your junk to someone else. And that's what good friends are for. They are there to be the hand of God and to offer you his forgiveness for your confession. So take some time to tell one another what you did that you now know is wrong, and then remind each other that God forgives you and wipes your slate clean. Then pray for each other. When you do, you will be actively living out God's Word and will for your life.

> Therefore, confess your sins to one another, and pray for one another so that you may be healed. The effective prayer of a righteous man can accomplish much.
>
> James 5:16

3. The New You. Now that you've gotten all that out of the way, the next thing is to decide who the new you is. In chapter 11 you made a list of things that will help you know how hot is too hot when it comes to your sexuality. Before you go on, have a look back at that list to remind yourself of your new commitment.,

After you do that, you will be ready to go on to make your commitment list for dressing. This is where you decide where you draw the line long before you have to shop for new clothes. It will help you shape your PR campaign all the more so that you won't buy stuff that doesn't gel with your new image.

MAKING THE COMMITMENT FOR "HOW HOT IS TOO HOT"

IS SEXY OKAY?

Here's your chance to make the commitment now to avoid sexy altogether. You've seen the facts, you've understood a guy's mind, and hopefully you've seen that sexy doesn't mesh with faith in God. It messes with people's minds and just confuses matters between the sexes. If you are ready to believe that, then make the commitment right now to avoid sexy by signing the statement below:

Father God, I understand that sexy is not fitting for my faith and so today I decide to avoid sexy altogether.

Signed _____

ONCE YOU'VE SIGNED YOUR NAME AND MADE THE COMMITMENT TO GOD, TAKE THE NEXT STEP AND GET PRACTICAL.
DECIDE

Save Sexy
for Your Husband

Once you're married sexy is not only okay, it's part of the marriage relationship. Assuming you aren't married right now you have no need to be sexy, but make no mistake, being married will be your chance to be sexy, for one man and one man only. So save your sexy shopping sprees for your future husband's credit card!

HOW HOT IS TOO HOT. LET'S BREAK IT DOWN:

THE TOP PART OF YOU

How hot is too hot for your top parts? Where do you draw the line?

How far down will your neckline go, and how far up will your shirt line come? Look at the model and draw your lines. These are where you won't go past. This is how hot is too hot.

THE BOTTOM PART OF YOU

Now it's time for the bottom part of you. How much of your bottom is too much? Where do you draw the line for undies showing and legs showing? There has to be a line that you think won't get guys all riled up—where is it? Go back to your model and draw the line for the top of your pants. And draw one for the bottom of your skirts. How far is too far?

Okay, now this is your model. This is what tells you what you own that's in and what you own that's out.

THE COMMITMENT

What part of you is sexy and what part of you is safe? Figure out with your friends where the line needs to be drawn and then make this commitment together:

Dear God, I commit to living up to my "how hot is too hot" rules. I want to be holy, and I want to be proper. I don't want to lead guys on anymore or cause any of them to stumble. So when it comes to my PR campaign, I commit to the following: I will use this model as my guide when trying on and buying clothes. I will keep the following parts of me covered up at all times, and I won't draw attention to them with body art or sexy clothes:

_____

_____

_____

_____

_____

Today, in front of God and these witnesses, I commit to honoring my body and the Creator of my body by covering up. I will no longer use my body as a tool to get the attention of guys. I want to be modest and holy. Thank you, God, for showing me the way.
Amen

Congrats! You've done it. You've made the commitment to protect yourself and the hearts and spirits of the guys and men around you. Bravo! Now get to it. Find clothes that work for the new you. Design your look, define your image, find hats at thrift stores, wear dresses over jeans, be daring, and be brave. Stick to your commitment and hold your friends accountable to theirs. Congratulations!

chapter 13

Invite your friends.

As I said earlier, I hope you have been going through this book with a friend or two, but if not, it's not too late to start. For this chapter you are going to have a Dressing Party. What's that, you ask? Well, it's a fashion show of sorts. What I want you to do is get a friend or two together and show off your wardrobe. Do a fashion show of all your stuff and talk about each item. How does it fit with your new PR campaign? Do you think guys are going to be all hot and bothered seeing you in it? Is the old man down the street drooling every time you walk by in this particular skirt?

Pull out all the stops. It's like doing a *What Not to Wear* party for your wardrobe. Nothing should be left out. You and your friends can make popcorn, put on some funky tunes, and do a little show, just for girls. You might even want to invite an adult, maybe a youth leader or a female youth pastor—someone who can help you make those hard calls on the stuff you really, really like that just isn't compatible with your new way of thinking and dressing. This isn't a time to go all Amish on me and throw out everything but turtlenecks and baggy pants; you still need to look girlish and cute. You still have a right to love your clothes—just be smart about them. Which ones show off too much skin? Which ones will lead guys and men down a path of destruction?

Also look for fun ways to mix things you might never have thought of. Take a look at some of these examples that will make you cute without drawing all eyes to your skin:

Spaghetti-strap top too revealing? Add a little T-shirt underneath to cover up your cleavage.

Pants too low waisted, showing off your sexy belly? Why not put a dress over the top of your pants? They can make great funky tops that no one else will have.

Skirt too short? Why not try it on over some of those tight jeans? It will cover up your sexy behind and make your legs look really long.

Layer, layer, layer! A lot of things don't have to be thrown away if you just think of ways to layer them. Put a long-sleeved tee under your short baby doll tee to cover up your stomach.

Get creative. The cutest girls who make the big-gest statement are girls who experiment with clothes. The key is really just to always be wearing something unique. A funky hat or weird shoes will set you off better than low-rise pants and a tank top. Think about adding personality to your wardrobe by going to a thrift store and buying something funky. Think 1970s, or pick another era that you like. There are all kinds of ways to be totally cute and not compromise on your image. So get a group together, do your dressing party, and check out new ways to be really cute without being sexy.

WRAPPING IT UP

Well, the end is here. Hopefully you've enjoyed our journey. The plan from the beginning of this book was to help you to create an image you can be proud of. My hope is that you have done or are doing it. Don't worry if it seems like too big of an endeavor or if things get in your way—like finding cool clothes that aren't too sexy. It might be hard at times, but it will be worth it when you commit yourself and your body to your God and determine to care for the things he cares for. Don't let yourself get frustrated. I know from experience that there will be days when you say "it's just too hard." But those days will pass when you finally find a style that suits you perfectly or a top that covers you completely without being dorky. I can remember going from store to store looking for something—anything—that wouldn't be sexy but would still be totally cute. It took me lots of tries, but eventually I found a piece here and there that said "Hayley." And now, over time, I've come to create an image of myself that I am proud of. I think I look unique and cool without looking sexy. I work hard at finding the right stuff but it's totally worth it. I search thrift stores and discount places 'til I'm dizzy, but in the end I'm happy, and I hope you are too. So dive into setting your perfect image and don't forget to have fun along the way!!

Notes

1. http://en.thinkexist.com/quotation/shelookedasifshehadbeenpoured intoher/217899.html.

2. Excerpt taken from *Dateable: Are You? Are They?* by Justin Lookadoo and Hayley DiMarco (Grand Rapids: Revell, 2003), 109.

3. http://en.thinkexist.com/quotation/ifmostofusareashamedofshabby clothesand/220925.html.

4. http://library.adoption.com/Parenting-Girls/Putting-it-all-Together-Is-Body-Piercing-Safe/article/6608/1.html.

5. Statistics on plastic surgery and liposuction are from Alissa Quart, *Branded: The Buying and Selling of Teenagers* (New York: Perseus Publishing, 2003).

6. The American Society of Plastic Surgeons, http://www.plasticsurgery .org/public_education/2000statistics.cfm.

7. *Merriam-Webster's Collegiate Dictionary*, 10th ed.

8. Ibid.

9. http://www.factsontap.org/factsontap/risky/the_facts.htm.

10. http://www.factsontap.org/factsontap/risky/discrimination.htm.

Ditch **MEAN** for good
with help from Hayley!

Available at your local bookstore

what is TECHNICALLY pure?

www.revellbooks.com

www.hungryplanet.net

www.ifuse.com

Hayley DiMarco writes cutting-edge books including *Mean Girls: Facing Your Beauty Turned Beast, Marriable*, the best-selling *Dateable: Are You? Are They?, The Dateable Rules*, and *The Dirt on Breaking Up*. Her goal is to give practical answers for life's problems and encourage girls to form stronger spiritual lives. From traveling the world with a French theater troupe to working for a little shoe company called Nike and then being the idea girl behind the success of the Biblezine *Revolve*, Hayley has seen a lot of life and decided to make a difference in her world. Hayley founded Hungry Planet, a think tank that feeds the world's appetite for truth. Hungry Planet helps organizations understand and reach the postmodern generation, while Hungry Planet books tackle life's everyday issues with a distinctly modern spiritual voice.

To keep the conversation going, log onto
www.howhotis2hot.com.

And for more on Hayley's other books check out
www.hungryplanet.net.

Hungry Planet

Feeding the world's appetite for truth.

Nine Straight Teen Titles on the CBA Young Adult Bestseller List

More than *800,000 Books in Print*

Three finalists and *one winner* of the ECPA Christian Book Awards

After all this and more, Hungry Planet has established itself as the leading provider of books for teens and not-yet-old adults. Dedicated to creating relevant, spiritually-based books, Hungry Planet delivers honest, in-your-face truth and 21st century application within a visually engaging package no reader can forget.

Award winning & bestselling books

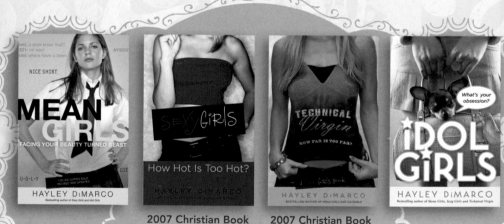

2007 Christian Book Award Winner!

2007 Christian Book Award Finalist!

Writing as a big-sister mentor, Hayley gives teen girls a biblical perspective on modesty, purity, friendship, and obsession.

Available at bookstores everywhere. To order, call 1-800-877-2665.

R Revell
www.revellbooks.com

Hayley and connect on Hungry Planet's social community, www.iFuse.com.